Jesus Knows

What does Jesus say
him in John 10:

MW00882591

Connect the dots ● 1-10. Color 🖍 the picture.

School Zone Publishing Company 02122

Bible Dot-to-Dot Numbers 1-25

A New King

What was David anointed as
in 2 Samuel 2:4 by the men of Judah?

Connect the dots ● 1–10. Color ✏ the picture.

4●　　　　　6●

2●　　　　　　　　　　8●

3●　　　5●　　　7●

1★—●10　　　　●9

Jesus will give you a crown that will last forever!

A Promise Kept

Who was born to Abraham in Genesis 21
when he was very old?

Connect the dots • 1–10. Color the picture.

Gold, Incense, and Myrrh

What did the Magi bring to
Jesus in Matthew 2:11?

Connect the dots ● 1–10. Color  the picture.

You can bring Jesus gifts from your heart!

Staying Faithful

Ruth stayed with Naomi. Boaz allowed
her to do this in Ruth 1 and 2.

Connect the dots • 1–10. Color the picture.

Shine Brightly

What does God in Psalm 18:28 turn your darkness into?

Connect the dots ● 1–15. Color  the picture.

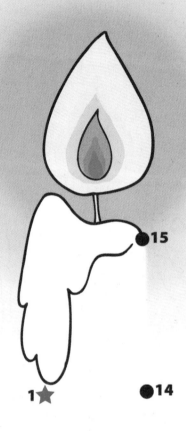

● 15

1 ★

● 14

● 11

3 ●

● 10

2 ● _____ ● 13

● 12

● 9

4 ●

● 7

● 8

5 ●   ● 6

Bible Dot-to-Dot Numbers 1-25 · © School Zone Publishing Company 02122

God's Word

What was written in Romans 15:4 to teach us
about God and give us hope?

Connect the dots ● 1–15. Color the picture.

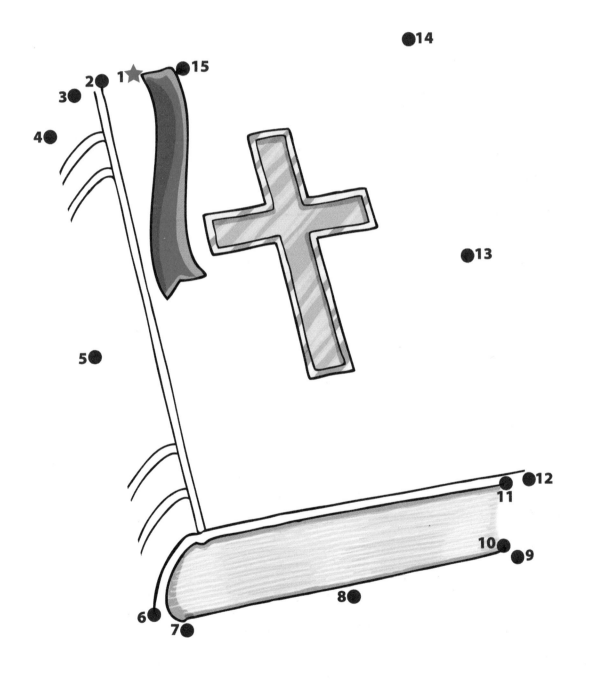

God's Special Helpers

Who will God command in Psalm 91:11 to
guard you in all of your ways?

Connect the dots ● 1–15. Color ✏ the picture.

Quite a Dream

What did Jacob see in a dream in Genesis 28:12
that reached all the way to heaven?

Connect the dots ● 1–15. Color ✏ the picture.

God can speak to you in your dreams!

One Hump or Two?

What in Mark 1:6 was John the Baptist's
coat made from?

Connect the dots ● 1–15. Color the picture.

God created every animal differently!

Going to Heaven

Who was taken up to heaven in Luke 24:51?

Connect the dots • 1–15. Color the picture.

Jesus is in heaven preparing a room just for you!

40 Days and 40 Nights

What did God use in Genesis 7:17 to keep
Noah's family safe in the flood?

Connect the dots ● 1–15. Color the picture.

God's love will always keep you safe!

Bible Dot-to-Dot Numbers 1-25

King of All

What of Judah is Jesus called
in Revelation 5:5?

Connect the dots • 1–15. Color the picture.

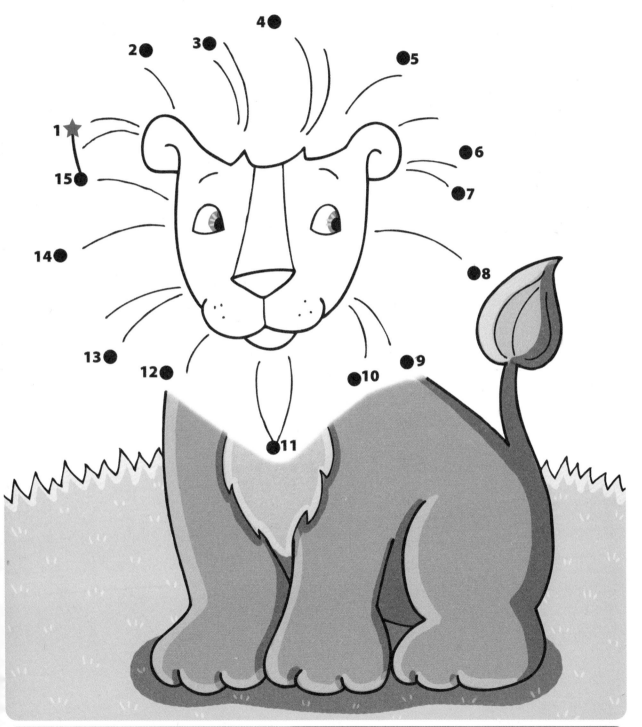

Jesus is the Lion of Judah—King of all!

The Third Day

What in Matthew 28:2 did an angel
roll away at the tomb?

Connect the dots • 1–20. Color the picture.

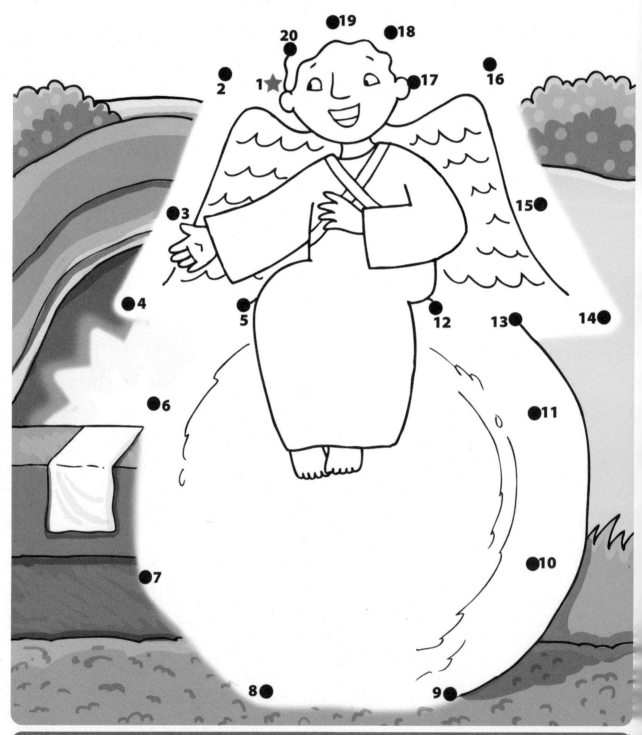

Pretty Birds

What is one of the beautiful birds God
created in Genesis 1:20?

Connect the dots • 1–20. Color ✏ the picture.

A Special Girl

What did Esther become in Esther 2:17 and 18
because she pleased the king?

Connect the dots ● 1–20. Color ✏ the picture.

Your faith is pleasing to God!

Bible Dot-to-Dot Numbers 1-25

A Talking Flame

What did Moses see in Exodus 3:2–4
when he heard God's voice?

Connect the dots ● 1–20. Color ✏ the picture.

God speaks to you in many different ways!

Divided Water

Who stretched out his hands as God commanded in Exodus 14 so the people could walk through the sea on dry land?

Connect the dots • 1–20. Color the picture.

God will keep you safe in his love!

Good News

Who did God send in Luke 2:1–13 to tell the shepherds about his son's birth?

Connect the dots ● 1–20. Color ✏ the picture.

You can proclaim the story of Jesus' birth, too!

A False Idol

What did Aaron build in Exodus 32:1-8
that displeased God?

Connect the dots ● 1–20. Color ✏ the picture.

6

7 9

4 5 8

3 8

2 10

1 11

20

19 18 15 14

17 16 13 12

Bible Dot-to-Dot Numbers 1-25 © School Zone Publishing Company 0212

A New Creation

What is used to symbolize "the old has gone and the new has come" from 2 Corinthians 5:17?

Connect the dots ● 1–25. Color the picture.

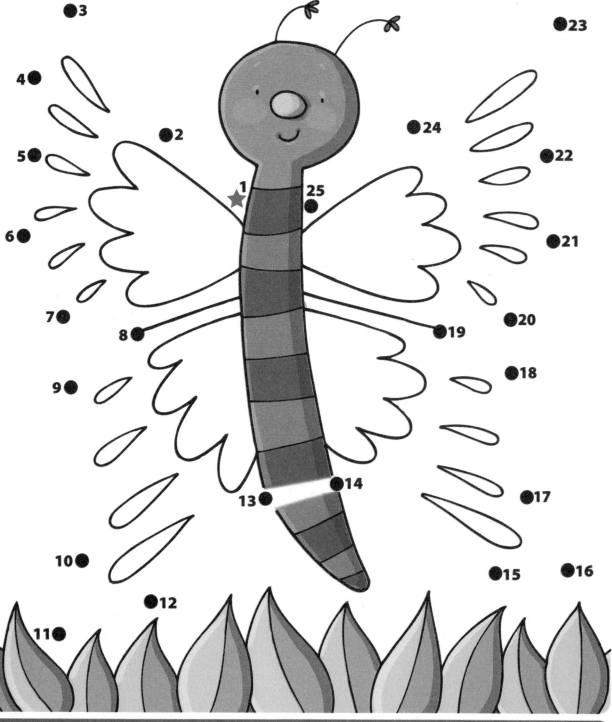

In Christ you are a new creation!

Let Them Come

Who did Jesus call to him in Luke 18:16 because
the kingdom of God belongs to them?

Connect the dots • 1–25. Color the picture.

Jesus loves all the children of the world!

Bible Dot-to-Dot Numbers 1-25

Wonderful Riches

What did Jesus say in Matthew 13:44 the
kingdom of heaven is like?

Connect the dots • 1–25. Color the picture.

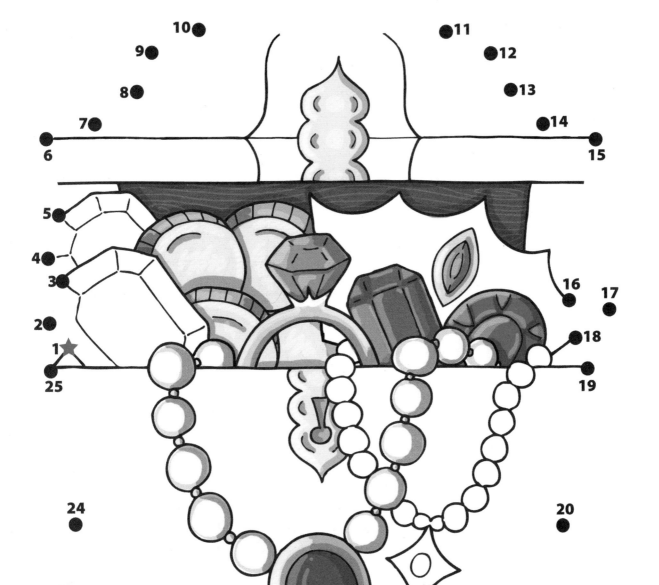

He Gave His All

What happened to Jesus in Luke 23:33 that took away your sins?

Connect the dots ● 1–25. Color ✏ the picture.

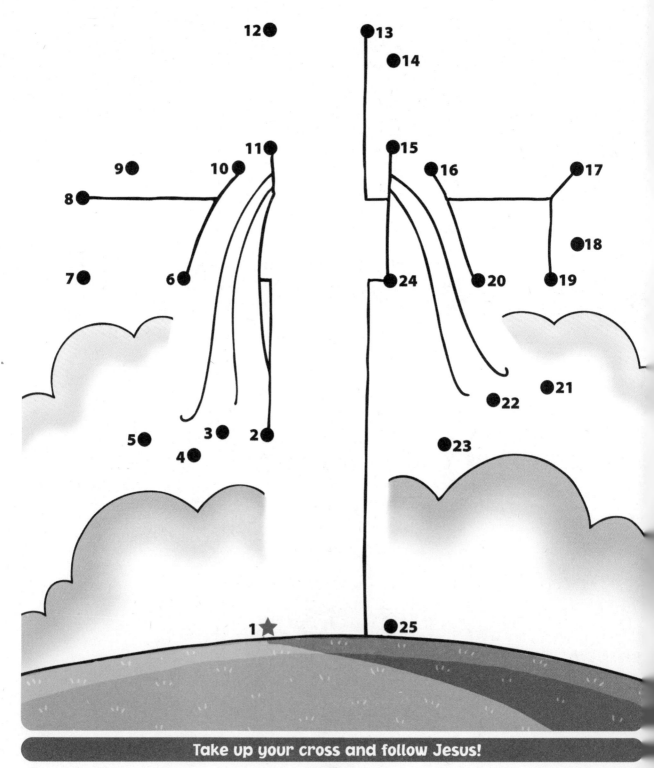

Take up your cross and follow Jesus!

Who Said That?

What did God use in Numbers 22:27-35
to speak to Balaam?

Connect the dots • 1-25. Color the picture.

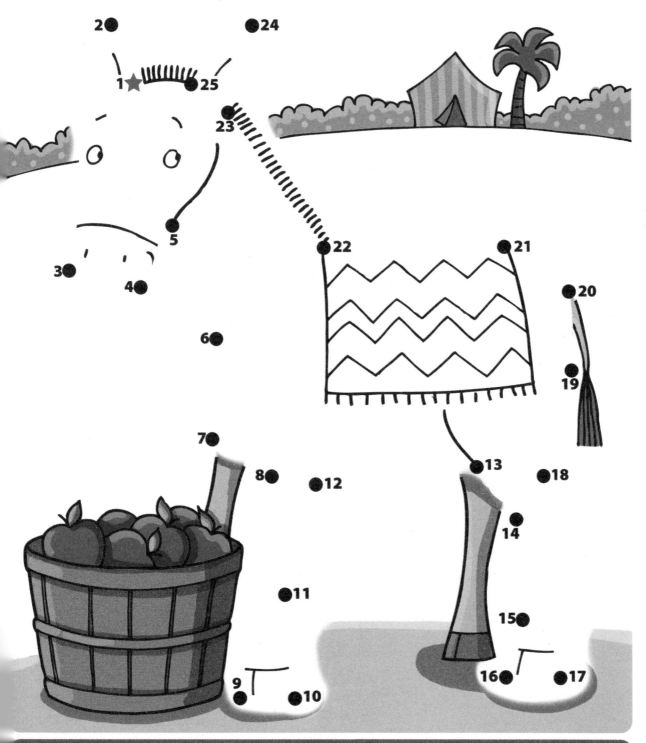

God's love is gentle and kind!

One Hot Spot

What in Daniel 3:8–30 were Shadrach, Meshach, and Abednego thrown into for believing in God?

Connect the dots • 1–25. Color the picture.

Stand firm in your faith!

Triumphant Entry

Who in Matthew 21:1-11 was riding a
donkey into Jerusalem?

Connect the dots • 1–25. Color the picture.

Hosanna! Blessed is he who comes in the name of the Lord!

27

A Special Delivery
What brought bread and meat to feed Elijah in 1 Kings 17:6?

Connect the dots ● 1–25. Color  the picture.

●25
1 ★

24 ●23

●22
●21
20 ●20
3● 2● ●17 ●19
●16
9 18●
10● ●15
11● 14●
12● 13

5● 4● 7●
6● 8●

Bible Dot-to-Dot Numbers 1-25   © School Zone Publishing Company 02

Two by Two

What went onto the ark in Genesis 6:19
male and female as God instructed?

Connect the dots ● 1–25. Color the picture.

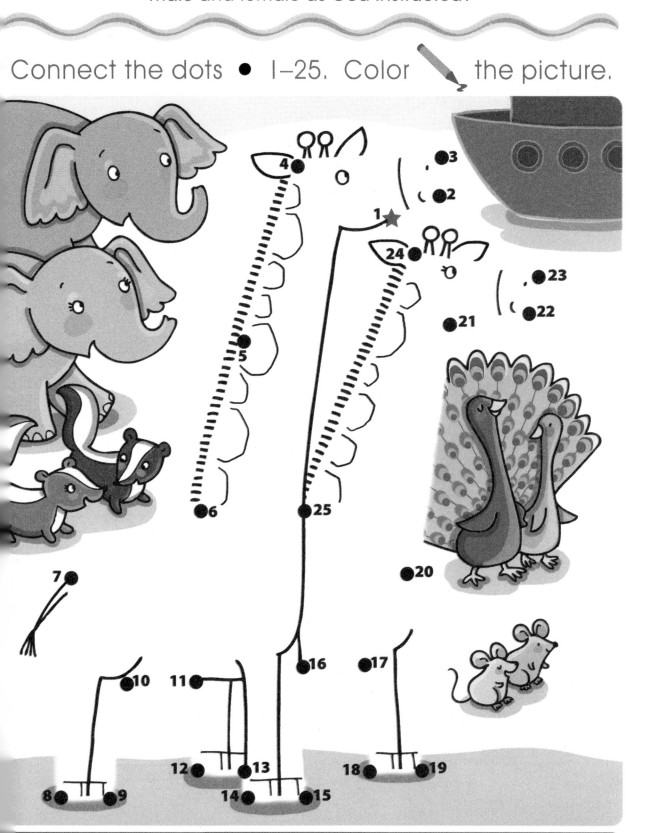

God keeps his promises!

A Special Table

What did Gideon build in Judges 6:24
that he called The Lord Is Peace?

Connect the dots ● 1–25. Color the picture.

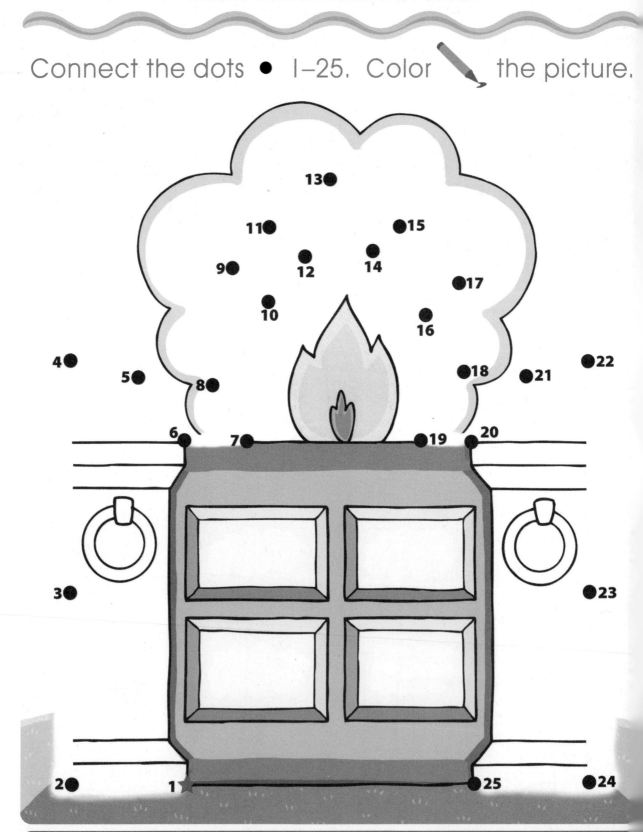

God is your Lord of Peace!

Preparing the Way

Who was the man in Matthew 3:1-6 who
prepared the way for Jesus?

Connect the dots ● 1-25. Color  the picture.

In Remembrance

What did Jesus do in Luke 22:19 and 20 that we
now do to remember him?

Connect the dots • 1–25. Color ✏ the picture.

Jesus gave his life on the cross for you!

Bible Dot-to-Dot Numbers 1-25 0212